'N Sync

Cynthia Laslo

Children's Press
A Division of Grolier Publishing
New York / London / Hong Kong / Sydney
Danbury, Connecticut

To Gladys, Veronique, and Claire—my favorite boy band!

Book Design: Nelson Sa
Contributing Editor: Jennifer Ceaser
Photo Credits: Cover © Tibor Bozi/Corbis; p. 4 © Lisa Rose/Globe Photos Inc.;
p. 6, © Tibor Bozi/Corbis; p. 9 © Kim Tonelli/Corbis; p. 10 © Lisa Rose/Globe
Photos Inc.; p. 13 © Henry McGee/Globe Photos Inc.; p. 14 © Tibor Bozi/Corbis;
pp. 17, 19 © Ethan Miller/Corbis; p. 20 © Tibor Bozi/Corbis; p. 25 © Henry
McGee/Globe Photos Inc.; p. 26 © Tibor Bozi/Corbis; p. 29 © Henry
McGee/Globe Photos Inc.; p. 30 © Tibor Bozi/Corbis; p. 33 © Henry
McGee/Globe Photos Inc.; p. 34 © Tibor Bozi/Corbis; p. 37 © Henry
McGee/Globe Photos Inc.; p. 38 © Fitzroy Barrett/Globe Photos Inc.; p. 40 ©
Ethan Miller/Corbis

Library of Congress Cataloging-in-Publication Data

Laslo, Cynthia, 1943-
    'N Sync / by Cynthia Laslo.
    p. cm. – (Celebrity bios)
    Includes bibliographical references and index.
    Summary: Describes the popular boy band 'N Sync, including information on
    each boy and a history of the group.
    ISBN 0-516-23324-6 (lib. bdg.) – 0-516-23524-9 (pbk.)
    1. 'N Sync (Musical group)—Juvenile literature. 2. Singers—United
States—Biography—Juvenile literature. [1. 'N Sync (Musical group) 2. Singers.]
    I. Title. II. Series.

ML3930.N3 L37 2000
782.42164'092'2—dc21
[B]
                                                        00-023321

CONTENTS

Introduction

'N Sync is one of the world's most exciting pop groups. These five talented and handsome young men have fans all over the globe. They have sold millions of records. They have performed with some of the world's biggest music stars, including Britney Spears, Janet Jackson, and Phil Collins.

How did 'N Sync get together? It's an exciting story. It's about chart-topping tunes. It's about dreams coming true. It's also about friendship, hard work, and talent.

The members of 'N Sync may be young, but fame didn't just happen overnight. It took many years for each of the members to build up his talent. To understand how 'N Sync made it big, it's important to know more about each of the guys in the group: Chris Kirkpatrick, Joey Fatone, Justin Timberlake, Lance Bass, and J. C. Chasez.

The members of 'N Sync from right to left: Lance Bass, Chris Kirkpatrick, Justin Timberlake, J. C. Chasez, Joey Fatone

CHAPTER ONE

How It All Began

"We know there are a million groups out there doing this. We know that the only way we're going to stand out and be around for a long time is by being ourselves."

— J. C. Chasez in *Jump*

In 1994, twenty-four-year-old Chris Kirkpatrick was working at Universal Studios theme park in Orlando, Florida. Chris had always dreamed of forming his own pop music group. One year later, he decided to make it a reality. Chris asked his friend, Joey Fatone, to be a part of the group. Joey immediately agreed. Chris and Joey brought in J. C. Chasez and Justin Timberlake, whom they had met during singing auditions (tryouts) in Orlando.

The four guys sounded great singing together, but something was missing. None of them felt secure singing the bass (deep) vocals. Justin called a former vocal coach he knew in Nashville. The coach suggested one of his own students, Lance Bass. Lance flew to Orlando to sing with the guys. It worked out immediately. Finally, after all of Chris's hard work, a singing group had been formed! The guys sounded great singing together. Now all they needed was a great name.

THE NAME GAME

How did 'N Sync get their name? Justin's mom was managing the group in their early days. She was trying to help them come up with a name for the group. They tried playing with the first initials of each other's names, but J J C L J didn't work. Justin's mom didn't give up! One day, she was looking at the last letters of each of the guys' names. Suddenly, she realized that it might work: JustiN, ChriS, JoeY, LansteN, (Lance's nick-name), and the second initial in J. C. The letters spelled N-S-Y-N-C ('N Sync), and the name stuck!

'N Sync got their name thanks to Justin's mom.

GETTING THEIR START

In 1995,'N Sync put together several demo tapes. A demo tape is a music recording made to present a group to a record label. 'N Sync had been together for about six months when music manager Lou Pearlman took an interest in the group. Pearlman alerted the producer Johnny Wright, a man who had put together New Kids On the Block and the Backstreet Boys. In 1996, with

In just two short years, 'N Sync became one of pop music's best-selling bands.

Pearlman's and Wright's help, 'N Sync signed a contract with BMG Records in Germany.

EARLY SUCCESS

In early 1996, 'N Sync's first album was released in Europe. 'N Sync worked on that album with the same music producers who had produced the hit Swedish group Ace of Base. The 'N Sync songs "I Want You Back" and "Tearin' Up My Heart" both were hit singles in Europe. The success of these songs led to two years of touring.

In April 1998, 'N Sync released the album *'N Sync* in the United States. At first, American sales of the album were disappointing. Then, in the summer of 1998, 'N Sync got a big break. The Backstreet Boys had to back out of a concert special for The Disney Channel. 'N Sync filled in for BSB, and the concert was a huge hit. The singles "I Want You Back" and "Tearin' Up My Heart" quickly climbed into the Top 10 on the music charts. 'N Sync videos were played constantly on MTV. *'N Sync* went multiplatinum, selling more than four million copies. 'N Sync also was earning millions of devoted fans all over the world.

CONTINUED SUCCESS

'N Sync was on its way to becoming one of pop music's biggest groups. In late 1998, they recorded the holiday album *Home For Christmas*.

They won two 1998 Billboard Video Music Awards for the video of "I Want You Back."

During 1998 and early 1999, 'N Sync toured with Janet Jackson and Britney Spears. In 1999, they went on the Boys of Summer tour and later headlined their own tour. They recorded hit singles with Phil Collins and Gloria Estefan. 'N Sync also won several awards that year: an American Music Award and a Blockbuster Award for Favorite New Artist, as well as a Teen Choice Award for Album of the Year for *'N Sync*.

'N Sync's next record, *No Strings Attached,* was released in March 2000. It came out three months late, because of a lawsuit with their record label. Both the first single, "Bye, Bye, Bye," and the album were immediate hits. *No Strings Attached* quickly hit #1 on the pop music charts.

'N SYNC vs. BSB

In a business where there are a lot of other boy bands, there also is a lot of competition. 'N Sync

The guys from 'N Sync avoid comparing themselves to other boy bands, including the Backstreet Boys.

often is compared to the Backstreet Boys. It's true that both groups have five young, handsome members who are fantastic singers. But 'N Sync's members consider their look and sound to be unique.

"When we put our group together, I didn't even know who the Backstreet Boys were," Justin told *Teen People*. "We didn't want to be the next anybody. We wanted to be the first 'N Sync."

Name	Christopher Alan Kirkpatrick
Nicknames	Crazy, Lucky
Born	October 17, 1971
Birthplace	Pittsburgh, Pennsylvania
Sign	Libra
Eyes/Hair	Brown/Brown
Favorites	
Foods	Pizza, tacos, chocolate ice cream
Color	Silver
Movie Stars	Audrey Hepburn, Mel Gibson, Jackie Chan
Movie	*Mad Max*
Music	Beastie Boys, Michael Jackson, The Beatles
TV Shows	"South Park," "The Simpsons"
Sports	Football, basketball
Team	Pittsburgh Steelers (football)
Hobbies	In-line skating, martial arts, street hockey

CHAPTER TWO

Chris Kirkpatrick

"I don't think there's ever been a group like us. We're the first group to [do] hardcore dancing and singing, then sing a pretty ballad." — Chris in *Teen People*

There would be no 'N Sync if it hadn't been for Chris Kirkpatrick. Chris is the one who had the idea to put together a group. Music has been a part of his life for as long as he can remember.

Christopher Alan Kirkpatrick was born into a very musical family. His mother, Beverly Eustice, is a voice teacher. His grandfather was a bandleader, and his grandmother was an opera singer. Several of Chris's aunts and uncles are jazz, country, and rock singers. No one in the family was surprised when Chris showed a talent for singing, even as a small child.

THE YOUNG PERFORMER

When Chris was about two years old, his mother took him to see the musical *Man of La Mancha*. After seeing the show just once, young Chris had memorized two of the songs! A few months later, he started singing at family reunions.

It wasn't until the fifth grade that Chris started performing in front of people other than his family. He played the lead role in a high-school production of the musical *Oliver*. When Chris was in high school, he starred in many other musicals, including *South Pacific*. He also began playing the guitar, keyboard, and trombone. Yet somehow, Chris found time for sports. He played football throughout junior high and high school.

In 1990, Chris moved to Orlando, Florida, where his father lived. He attended nearby Valencia Community College. Chris began his college career studying theater and psychology, but he ended up majoring in music. He later graduated with an Associate of Arts degree.

Chris and Justin harmonize beautifully together.

Chris sang in small coffeehouses in the Orlando area while attending college. He also joined the Caroling Company, a group that performed songs professionally at Christmastime. In 1994, Chris got a job working at Universal Studios, a theme park in Orlando, Florida. His job was to sing in front of one of the park's restaurants. He sang doo-wop, which is a 1950s style of rock and roll music with a lot of harmonizing. Finally, in 1995, Chris fulfilled his dream of being part of a singing group—'N Sync.

ALL ABOUT CHRIS

Chris Kirkpatrick is the oldest member of 'N Sync. He is an excellent dancer, but he's most famous for his singing. Chris has a unique high voice, which is called a soprano.

Chris has a reputation for being the wild member of the group. He is always playing jokes and making people laugh. He does comedy routines and impersonates Cartman from the TV show "South Park." He likes to experiment with outrageous clothes and hairstyles.

Chris's sense of humor hides a more serious side. He is a very hardworking person. He recently started his own company, called FuMan Skeeto Enterprises. FuMan Skeeto is a corporation that produces new artists, designers and performers. The company also makes clothes, most of which are designed by Chris.

Chris and Justin perform during the 1999
"Ain't No Stopping Us Now" tour.

Name	**Justin Randall Timberlake**
Nicknames	Curly, Bounce, Baby
Born	January 31, 1981
Birthplace	Memphis, Tennessee
Sign	Aquarius
Eyes/Hair	Blue/Dirty Blond

Favorites

Food	His mom's Italian chicken with garlic
Color	Baby blue
Movie Stars	Sandra Bullock, Brad Pitt
Movies	*Scream, Twelve Monkeys, The Usual Suspects*
Music	Stevie Wonder, Jermaine Dupri
TV Shows	"Friends," "Seinfeld," "South Park"
Sports	Basketball
Hobby	Playing basketball

CHAPTER THREE

Justin Timberlake

"If I could talk, I could sing. I was always performing for somebody."

— Justin in *Teen People*

Justin Randall Timberlake was born in Memphis, Tennessee. Even at a very young age, Justin loved to sing and dance. He sang along with songs on the radio when he was only two years old!

Justin's parents encouraged him to follow his dreams of becoming a performer. Justin's father was a singer in a bluegrass band. Justin's family—including his grandmother, uncles, and aunts—all participated in church choirs. Justin credits his involvement in a church choir with helping him

Did you know?

Justin learned many of his dancing moves by watching Janet Jackson music videos.

to develop his singing skills.

When Justin was in the fourth grade, he entered a school talent contest with some other boys. They pretended to be New Kids On The Block and did a lip-sync performance of one of their songs. They did so well in the contest that girls chased them after they had finished the performance!

BIG BREAK

Justin's big break came when he was eleven years old. The television show "Star Search" came to Memphis to look for talented performers. Justin auditioned and was invited to perform on the show. "Star Search" flew him to their studios in Orlando, Florida. Justin decided to perform a country-and-western song on the show. Then he heard about an audition for Disney's "Mickey Mouse Club," which was taping in the same TV studio. Justin auditioned with thirty thousand other kids. He was one of the seven kids who were chosen to be in the cast!

Justin performed on the "Mickey Mouse Club" from 1992 to 1994. During that time, he met his first love, Britney Spears, who was also on the show. The two are no longer dating, but they remain good friends. Justin also made another good friend during that time—fellow Mousketeer J. C. Chasez. The two recorded several demo tapes together.

ALL ABOUT JUSTIN

Justin is the youngest member of 'N Sync. He also is the most athletic member of the group. Whenever Justin has free time, he is on the basketball court. He counts Michael Jordan as one of his idols. Justin keeps himself in terrific physical shape with all of the dancing he does on tour. He also does sets of 100 or more push-ups several times each day.

Justin's family is very important to him. His parents are divorced, but Justin is close to both sets of parents. "I call my stepdad 'Dad' and my natural dad 'Daddy,' " Justin told *Entertainment Teen*. Justin counts his mother, Lynn, as one of his best friends. No matter where Justin is in the world, he and his mom talk to each other several times a day on the phone. He also tries to spend as much time as he can with his two younger half-brothers, Jonathan and Steven.

In addition to singing and dancing, Justin has taken up acting. He has appeared on the sitcoms "Clueless" and "Sabrina, the Teenage Witch." He dyed his blond curls brown to play the part of a model in the Disney TV-movie "Model Behavior."

Justin also has started an organization that helps kids who want to learn more about the arts. The Justin Timberlake Foundation provides funds to kids who want to pursue art and music.

Justin is the youngest and tallest member of 'N Sync.

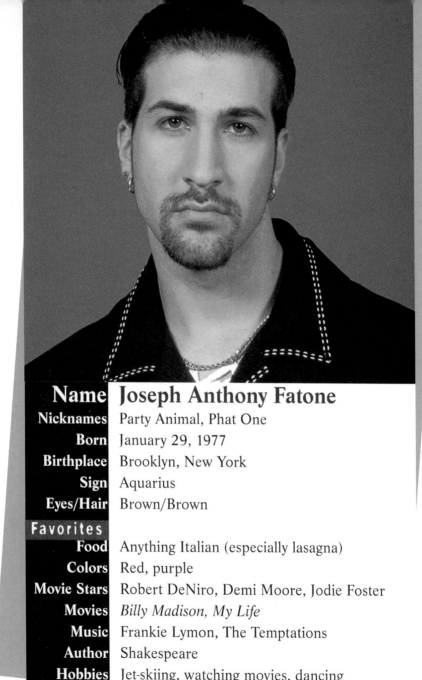

Name	Joseph Anthony Fatone
Nicknames	Party Animal, Phat One
Born	January 29, 1977
Birthplace	Brooklyn, New York
Sign	Aquarius
Eyes/Hair	Brown/Brown
Favorites	
Food	Anything Italian (especially lasagna)
Colors	Red, purple
Movie Stars	Robert DeNiro, Demi Moore, Jodie Foster
Movies	*Billy Madison, My Life*
Music	Frankie Lymon, The Temptations
Author	Shakespeare
Hobbies	Jet-skiing, watching movies, dancing

CHAPTER FOUR

Joey Fatone

"We love singing together. That's what came first. It wasn't about the image."
— Joey in *Teen People*

As did other members of 'N Sync, Joseph Anthony Fatone, Jr. grew up in a musical family. Joey's father, Joseph Sr., had been a doo-wop singer as a young man. Joseph Sr. encouraged his son's interest in music and performing.

As a boy, Joey sang in his church choir and in local a cappella groups. A cappella songs have singing and harmonizing, but no instrumental music. Joey also appeared in plays and musicals. His first onstage singing role was in a school production of the musical *Oklahoma!*

The Fatone family moved to Orlando when Joey was thirteen years old. He continued to perform in school musicals, including *West Side Story*. After high school, Joey got a job singing and dancing at Universal Studios. Chris Kirkpatrick was working there at the same time. Joey and Chris quickly became friends and, eventually, bandmates.

ALL ABOUT JOEY

One of Joey's favorite things about being in 'N Sync is all the traveling he gets to do. He loved when the band toured in Germany and Asia because he thought the scenery was so beautiful. He likes to videotape the band everywhere in the world that they go.

When he's not on tour, Joey still lives with his parents in Orlando. He lives in the same house he lived in as a teenager. Joey's parents are very

Lance and Joey perform together at an outdoor concert.

supportive of his singing career. His mom handles
'N Sync's fan mail, and his dad helps him to
make financial decisions. Talent also runs in the
family: Joey's older brother and sister perform at
Universal Studios.

Name	**James Lance Bass**
Nicknames	Lansten, Scoop, Mr. Cool
Born	May 4, 1979
Birthplace	Laurel, Mississippi
Sign	Taurus
Eyes/Hair	Green/Blond

Favorites

Foods	Mexican food, French toast
Colors	Red, blue
Movie Stars	Tom Hanks, Meg Ryan
Movies	*Armageddon, Clue*
Music	Garth Brooks, Brian McKnight
TV Shows	"Friends," "I Love Lucy"
Hobbies	Horseback riding, jet-skiing, rock climbing

CHAPTER FIVE

Lance Bass

"From day one, I knew [the band] was going to work. The first time we sang together, I was like, 'This is it.'"

— Lance in *Teen People*

Unlike the other members of 'N Sync, Lance Bass wasn't sure he would be a singer. He was a member of his church choir, but he didn't get serious about performing until he was fourteen years old. Lance was in the ninth grade when he went to his first concert—Garth Brooks. Lance was so impressed with the performance, he realized that he would enjoy being an entertainer, too.

Lance was the last member to join 'N Sync. He and Justin had happened to take voice lessons from the same vocal coach in Tennessee. While Chris was forming 'N Sync in Orlando, Justin called the former vocal coach to get his suggestion for someone who could sing the bass parts. The coach recommended Lance, who was flown to Orlando to meet the rest of the guys. They immediately hit it off, and 'N Sync finally became a group!

ALL ABOUT LANCE

Lance is a devoted Christian and a smart businessman. He is the most organized member of the group and is interested in music management. Lance started a music management company, Free Lance Entertainment, with his mother and sister. In fact, he's already managing the careers of two country singers, Jack Defeo and Meredith Edwards.

Lance is not only a singer, he's also an actor. His first role was on the TV show "7th Heaven,"

Lance is a singer, dancer, actor, and businessman who manages the careers of new singing artists.

in which he played the love interest of Beverly Mitchell's character. Lance impressed everyone on the set of "7th Heaven" with his awesome acting ability. From there, Lance went on to appear in a small role as a flight engineer in the movie *Jack of All Trades*. Lance is excited about acting, but he insists that music always will come first.

Name	Joshua Scott Chasez
Nicknames	J. C., Mr. Serious, Mr. Sleepy
Born	August 8, 1976
Birthplace	Washington, D.C.
Sign	Leo
Eyes/Hair	Blue/Brown

Favorites

Food	Chinese
Colors	Blue, orange
Movie Stars	Meg Ryan, Harrison Ford
Movies	All *Star Wars* and *Indiana Jones* films
Music	Seal, Sting, Brian McKnight
TV Show	"Party of Five"
Sports	Football
Team	Washington Redskins (football)
Hobbies	In-line skating, karate, swimming

CHAPTER SIX

J. C. Chasez

"I've always been a workaholic. Once I go into something, I dive into it with both feet."
— J. C. from 'N Sync: The Official Book

Joshua (J. C.) Scott Chasez was born on August 8, 1976. J. C.'s mother is a writer and editor. His father networks computers at the White House. Even at a young age, it was apparent that J. C. had a good singing voice. J. C. was shy, so his parents did not push him to perform.

Because he was so shy, J. C. didn't get a lot of experience as a performer. Eventually, a friend dared him to dance with some girls from school in a talent show. Twelve-year-old J. C. got up the nerve to dance, and the group wound up winning first place. They continued to do their act at other local talent shows, where they were a huge hit.

In 1989, J. C.'s mother saw an ad for auditions for the "Mickey Mouse Club." She suggested that J. C. try out for the show. He auditioned with five hundred other kids and was chosen to be part of the cast. J. C. was on the "Mickey Mouse Club" for four years. During that time, he became close with fellow cast members Justin Timberlake and Britney Spears. J. C. also appeared in the short-lived TV series "Emerald Cove."

After the "Mickey Mouse Club" was canceled in 1994, J. C. moved to Nashville and then to Orlando. He met up with Justin again and hung out with Joey Fatone. When 'N Sync was just getting started, J. C. was one of the first to join.

ALL ABOUT J. C.

J. C. is known as the most serious member of the group. He admits that he is a perfectionist who

J. C. is known as the most serious member of 'N Sync.

keeps a close eye on his goals. J. C. usually is the member of 'N Sync who gets the others to focus and concentrate on getting everything exactly right. He reminds the others to be on time for rehearsals.

J. C. also loves to travel. He enjoys performing in foreign cities for all kinds of people. He finds it interesting to experience different cultures. He loves to meet his fans from all over the world.

CHAPTER SEVEN

More Than Just Music

It's not all fun and games for 'N Sync. The guys constantly are working and touring. They write, rehearse, travel, and perform. Their workdays are very long. Sometimes they work for seventeen or eighteen hours without a break!

Another hard part of 'N Sync's success is that the guys are away from their families for long periods of time. Fortunately, each of them has family members that sometimes join them on tour. Joey's brother Steven often travels with 'N Sync to videotape their concerts. Lance works with his sister and his mother to manage new musicians. Justin, J. C., and Chris have family members that sometimes join them on tour, too.

'N Sync appears at a benefit for breast cancer research.

'N Sync is on tour for long periods of time, but the band still finds the time to get involved with charity causes.

'N SYNC GIVES BACK

The guys of 'N Sync feel that it's important to give back to the community whenever they can. So in 1999, the group started a program called Challenge for the Children. Its goal is to raise

money for children's programs and charities.
Each year, 'N Sync teams up with other sports
and entertainment stars to take part in The
Challenge for the Children Basketball Game.
The game benefits a number of different causes,
including the Arnold Palmer's Hospital for
Women and Children and the Atlanta Hawks
Foundation. 'N Sync also participates in the Stars
in the Wild project, which raises money for
endangered animals.

In May 2000, Lance competed on the game
show "Who Wants to be a Millionaire," along
with Queen Latifah, Rosie O'Donnell, and other
celebrities. Along with the other contestants,
Lance donated his winnings to charity.

'N Sync know that they are an inspiration to
millions of young people all over the world. The
band's continued success sets an example: with
hard work and determination, every young person can make his or her dreams come true.

TIMELINE

1995 • 'N Sync forms as a band.

1996 • 'N Sync signs a contract with BMG Records.
'N Sync's first album is released in Europe.

1997 • 'N Sync signs a contract with RCA Records.

1998 • 'N Sync appears in a July concert on The Disney Channel.
• The singles "Tearin' Up My Heart" and "I Want You Back" hit the Top 10.
• *'N Sync* goes multiplatinum.
• *Home For Christmas* is released in November.
• 'N Sync tours with Janet Jackson and Britney Spears.
• "Let the Music Hear Your Soul" is released to benefit disabled children.
• 'N Sync wins two Billboard Video Music Awards for "I Want You Back."

1999 • 'N Sync goes on the Boys of Summer tour.
• 'N Sync headlines their own tour.
• 'N Sync makes guest appearances on the TV shows "TRL," "Clueless," and "Sabrina, the Teenage Witch."

- 'N Sync performs for the 1999 Miss Teen USA pageant.
- 'N Sync performs at the Grand Ole Opry.
- 'N Sync records with Phil Collins for the soundtrack to the movie *Tarzan.*
- 'N Sync sings with Gloria Estefan on the song "Music of My Heart."
- 'N Sync wins a Blockbuster Award and an American Music Award for Favorite New Artist.
- *'N Sync* wins the Teen Choice Award for Favorite Album of the Year.
- 'N Sync signs with Jive Records.

2000
- The March release of *No Strings Attached* sells 3.76 million copies in its first three weeks and hits #1 on the charts.
- Justin is once again chosen as one of *Teen People's* Hottest Stars.
- 'N Sync sings the Oscar-nominated song, "Music of My Heart" at the Academy Awards.
- Lance is a contestant on the TV quiz show "Who Wants to Be a Millionarie."
- 'N Sync starts a worldwide tour in May.
- Justin appears in the movie "Model Behavior."
- 'N Sync appears in the movie *Jack of All Trades.*

NEW WORDS

a cappella singing without instruments

audition a tryout performance

bass the lowest adult male singing voice

chart a listing that ranks music sales

choreographer someone who creates dance moves to go along with music

country-and-western music imitating the folk style of the southern United States or the western cowboy

demo tape a music recording made to present a song to a record label

doo-wop a vocal style of rock and roll, usually done a cappella

harmony combination of musical notes sung at the same time

headline to be the main act, instead of the opening act, of a concert

lip-synch to pretend to sing along with a recording of a song

multiplatinum a record that sells at least three million copies

musical a play with singing and dancing

opera a drama set to music and made up of vocal pieces and orchestra music

pop music relating to popular music, as in "pop singer"

producer the person who supervises or finances the production of an album, film, or television program

record label a company that produces and sells records

recording studio an area where music is recorded and produced

sitcom a comedy TV show, usually thirty minutes in length

soprano the highest range of singing voice

FOR FURTHER READING

Adams, Ashley. *'N Sync*. New York: Omnibus Press, 1999.

Nichols, Angie. *'N Sync Confidential*. New York: BPI Communications, Inc., 1999.

'N Sync and K. M. Squires. *'N Sync: The Official Book*. New York: Bantam Doubleday Dell Books for Young Readers, 1998.

Netter, Matt. *'N Sync: Tearin' Up the Charts*. New York: Pocket Books, 1999.

RESOURCES

FuMan Skeeto
www.fumanskeeto.com
The official site of Chris's clothing line. All items are available for purchase. The site contains pictures of clothing and accessories, including hard-to-find items.

The Official 'N Sync Web Site
www.nsync.com
This official site contains audio clips, lyrics, bios of each member, and photos. You also can chat with other fans in the chat room.

Wall of Sound
www.wallofsound.go.com/artists/nsync/home.html
This site shows the history of the band's beginnings, including their performing experiences. It also has links to bands 'N Sync has performed with, and publications in which they've appeared.

INDEX

ABOUT THE AUTHOR

Cynthia Laslo was born in Norway and moved to Iowa with her parents in 1955. After high school, she taught English as a second language in the school system of Maricao, Puerto Rico.